The Diary of Saint Marion

(Found in a laundry basket in Hamtramck, Detroit, 1971)

Gloria Monaghan

LILY POETRY REVIEW BOOKS

For my grandmother, Marion Elizabeth Flewelling Navin
&
Violet and Josephine

Table of Contents

Relics

Opera Bag

Black of course and miniature
clasp in superb condition leather as thin
as coarse paper. Couldn't have held much more
than a few coins for tipping a bathroom attendant
or purchasing milk.

I don't know whether I tell
the truth about the beauty of what is lost.

The purse itself, soft cowhide black inked.

Cigarettes and Desire

I'm going ashore tonight to see some show- I'm tired, lonely and disgusted
USS Mississippi, 1919

From the crow cawing outside the window, I
learned that Mary, Joseph and Jesus,
lost in the Great War,
moved to the city of angels
for the romantic sun.

All my hopes departed at noon.

Forgive this scrawl.

If You Can Grow on a Tree

You can grow anywhere,
oaknut
cascading from the tree,
attached permanently to a stick.

You are fallen, halved, exposed, unflowered, unleafed-
a shell, but within the shell a sunset.
The cupule outlined by a red maple crust
under that, a black line.
The interior is a soft hazelnut yellow
where the green plumule seed sat;
now there is a universe,
an orange halved
bursting with directional seeds
a microcosm of the tree.

Circles of forever; you are there,
young nut, with your ancestors
each one has a handprint on your soul.

I Love a Motel in June, Don't You?

(written in St. Marion's father's handwriting on the back of an old polaroid)

My parents had a Volkswagen and drove across the country
to get married, listening to the radio.
I had a feeling this happened with the same carelessness
as when you witness a crime and are silent
and simply move forward with whatever
it was you were doing: feeding the cats,
brewing coffee, pulling up the blinds.

Shape, shape come to me bend
like a panther down and take my face into
your hands. Make me aware of something beyond
the cat bowl and filament of
dust on the venetian blind.
Make me obvious
to the trees, the bright pavement
and grey day.
                  Obscurity moon, are
you listening?

Adorned with a Picnic Hat
in the Black and White Photo

Perhaps your father gave it to you.
You wore it in the off season unaware
that it is called a picnic hat
for a reason.

Drunken smile,
cigar in your mouth
perhaps the ash fell against your pant leg
like an old wound.
                    Father perennially gone.

The fairy who lifted his soul up to heaven
found you in a bar in Windsor.
You both smiled under the Ambassador Bridge
in a green sailboat you made out of wood
on Saturdays in the garage
until it all closed in
and the fairy left town for good.

The Chalice

Nut Island, Hough's Neck

Hough's Tomb around the corner from the sewage
treatment plant and guard house
at the end of Sea Street.

The pier is scattered with the flat husks of oysters.
Dead low tide, gulls and ducks murmur in small water
besides their occasional squall,
a gentle drop and pang of a shell deliberate
from the webbed feet; a momentary release
oyster, or clam
to the preferred flat stone
the dive down for the catch.

Between the divine orange
sun and luminous blue
is the outlined eye of a teenage gull
surveying his kingdom.

Winter Solstice

Beauty itself brings copies of itself,
in her gold cloak offering refuge.
One thing I asked was to dwell
in the house of the Lord,
to stay, to tarry
stun and perplex
all origins of the word.

Thy face Lord, I will seek.

A Christmas star last appeared
the year St. Francis died.

Hope had grown grey hairs.
Hope had mourning on.
Hope had a star for a face.

On the winter solstice, Sister Mary died.
A giant winter moon held
the fewest hours of daylight.

A bell awakened and told us,
someone good has died.

Discretion is the Better Part of Valor

(Shakespeare, Henry IV)

Acorns of oaks, the top is a cupule,
then the fruit wall.
He called his son a fruit,

then the remains of style, the innermost whorl of the flower
the gynoecium, the woman house,
within that the embryo, the seed.

The old man raised his cane
above his son's head
called him a *faggot*.

The son caught the cane and said,
never again will you raise your hand
against my head.

They called your father Jesus.
As if they could baptize him in holy water,
wash him clean of his own father's sins.

But the rite never did happen
and when the house was destroyed, the bedroom furniture,
broken, he went to a motel.

The Man Who Did Not Believe in Watches

After Yusef Komunyakaa

For a minute he let me stay, drifting away
that autumn day after his father hit him senseless,
old familiar betrayal.

Eventually, away from all of them, an internal explosion.
I've seen it before (that is after)
in the vacancy of green eyes.

He set himself on fire
on a dry day in October when the last of the small green leaves
hung tenacious, and dark branches
said, *may I? and can you?*

Twinning Acorns

Mark yourself a hero. Emerge.
Let the fine dust settle on your green leaves
and liken that life to shelf life.
You find that your neighborhood
is a garden, with black wrought iron fences,
marigolds and dogs and the dappled light
that falls gentle on your face.

Dream,
tiny capped stranger, you will see
as you grow the world crooked and willful as dirt
(Hide your eyes. Do not look.) It is too hard
to watch someone else suffer
in dirt.

I Am Not Afraid of Storms

I am not afraid of storms
or the wind or moving fragment against
sky in mid-winter, or early December
wandering sky
of blown leaves against the new wet snow
or *your* face, the one I imagined as we all imagine.
The one face that will save me.

He gets up and moves towards me,
and I put down the book
I was pretending to read.
(Dickens, *Middlemarch*, Bronte or was it Ford Maddox Ford)
From the café car, the two of us make our ways to passenger seats.
I have my kewpie doll my cousin gave me for luck,
and we will do nothing but talk into the night
all the way to Syracuse. We will not even kiss.
It is exactly like the stars against the night sky.

Better this way, so when he gets off at Syracuse,
I don't have to say goodbye.
He didn't really want me with all his heart.
The leaves stick to the new snow and ice
and yes, even died.

I am not afraid of storms because I like them.
I feel safe indoors, but I do worry over the tulip tree
if it will split open and crash into the house.
I hugged the tulip tree
as if it could divide me, and I would be a fig again
with meticulous seeds and divine divides,
stickiness inherent in my veins
like the callow lies of my grandfather,

his pig skinned key holder of two centuries skeletal to Sargent,
sailor to hawking product for Ford.
What became of him, green-eyed boy?
Oh captain, mon Lieutenant captain?

I am not afraid of storms, but I do wonder
how I will die.
            Sister Ida said; what is the cat thinking?
I said I don't know, but he doesn't stay sad for long
and this is true. I know nothing of the mouse.

At the Motherhouse, Senior Living

All night the sound of mother's cane
rising out of bed to go to the bathroom.
Waking to the smell of lilies
and the small sound of the cane tapping,
methodically to the bathroom.

This is in Monroe where the trees turn slowly
to gold from green
and a faint orange rust leaks into the sunset.

Arrowhead, Squantum

There in the green marsh pond on the other side of Wollaston
where the Native Americans negotiated and were later mostly wiped
out in 1716,
where a disease like Scarlet Fever, or an epidemic
took most of the Ponkapoag people
who ate salmon, eels, herring and scallops foraged the beach
waiting for June and July to hold council.

I can hear them still pine on the hummock
in the deep, moss color of the pond across from the ocean.
The light in the sky reflects the endless loss
of a milk green dream to get lost in.

*Hummock is a Native American site and the original name of the tribe (now Massachusetts) in the region. The wooded hummock in Squantum is formally recognized as historic by descendants of the Ponkapoag people.

Saint Marion's Promise

A dragonfly shimmered on a leaf
on the Pamet River on a Sunday in July.
In spite of the heat, I drew down
like a careful botanist,
on my haunches for a better look
at the green and blue of his body.
His black eyes looked me over like Edward G. Robinson;
his silver tongue flickered in the soft breeze.
The green river was so smooth. You could cut it with a butter knife.

Garage

It is planting time and still cold in the garden
where I left the cat leash in the clover.
There doesn't seem to be enough green,
or plants; we need more of those and more
rattan chairs: cushionless, faded, and outlined
in dark teal unraveling beneath the tulip tree.

In the dark night when dreams come, I wake,
fingers clutched, going over the same routine
the one where I say, *OK, this is it,*
except somehow I get convinced to stay,
grab the small animal to my chest, whispering.

Unexpectedly grandmother's brown spotted
hands come to mind.
Her old gardening tools, pruning shears and trowel
smell of dirt and must in the garage.
Her own mother's gardening gloves lie in the rusted iron bowl.

But in the garage, it's voice without voice, God's voice
in petunias, dirt, peat moss, and geraniums.
Help me plant, I say to the silence.

The Origin Story of Saint Marion

Was I a spoiled Victorian child
in the dress of the day flounced white gown
and cap, with a cowlick
flattened against my forehead slightly
downturned smile, not a frown,and quite
large brown eyes that were from birth
slightly sad, slightly in awe
of this magnificent earth?

The only child of Frank,
the butcher and his wife, Maude.

A farm girl in city finery,
as if my mother knew I would be different,
be carried away downriver
past Monroe, past Saginaw, past Dearborn
to a Detroit 3rd Avenue boarding house.

Later, up in the convent in Monroe,
with the IHM sisters praying,
I converted at 63.

And then a century ended
with a lions' roar in a dark room of men smoking old cigars,
and the butcher with blood on his hands from the spring lamb?

                    What hand pushes back
the adolescent hair from your face
so you can finally sleep against the evening?

A mother
saying *shhhh*
don't cry; think of something sweet.

For Martha
and Sister Janina

Dear Reader, Before I Write, I'll Tell You About Martha

Father Edward, he was no priest, but a man with wives, (that is what his maid said.)
Friday, 1907, baking day, in the village of Isadore, Sister Janina disappeared.
11 years later, Father Edward Podlaszewski, the new priest, built a church on the site.
He had heard rumors from Bishop Kozlowski and asked the sexton, Jacob Flees, to
     assist.
That late fall night with lanterns and a potato fork in hand, they lifted Sister's
bones into a wooden crate with remains of a fetus cradled in her skeleton.

Father Edward was called to the Miller home. Martha, my friend,
was the teenage
daughter who worked as a housekeeper at Holy Rosary church.
She was pregnant by Father Edward. Only I knew.

Martha still remembers Sister Janina, who often
sang behind the wooded pine. On her last day, Sister Janina
left her rosary and her prayer book on her chipped window sill.

Cupboard Love Loyalty

In the Mojave Desert, a man called George Van Tassel
tried to build a time machine,

and Martha snorted in an effort to catch hold
of her breath

before letting go of reason, obligation
and her tax refund

and the cupboard love.

Martha the Country Insomniac

Martha had years of waiting on the curb
for the mother to arrive
in her destroyed car
to claim her child,
school out hours before.
In the library with Jack London, until even that shut down.
Or watching Candy swim, until even the swimmers
had toweled dry in the five o'clock sun,
or until the wild reeds were harvested away from grain.

Deliberate the day,
the space between her sneaker and the street.
There she is suddenly
cat in car; there she is.

Walk to School with Martha

We used to walk to school together
and would pretend we lived on Cherry Street
instead of Hannah.
                      We lollygagged
and sang.

One time she showed me her report card with every subject failing.
I remember trying to learn to read music.
My name was called on the PA for winning chocolates,
that is when I knew it was all a dream.

Garland Pose

Martha squatted, Malasana.
Her body alignment told her
there was a real possibility of being fired.
She calculated her savings.
Her daughter's room became a refuge of the orange sun.

Refusing to collapse in fear, she dialed an ancestor
and went to the ocean.
Waves came in succession of each other
grey eared soft, like the grey dawn
in Ulysses' return.

She waited for a seal to bring her good news.
This year the green dune grass has been kissed
with yellow sun
and the morning is like no other.

Car Thief

Elle a trop de Maquillage, Elle doit être un Voleur de Voitures
(She has too much makeup on, she must be a car thief.)

Martha's brother drove the car himself.
I put her in the back. It was a two-car process.
When moving something hot on the seat to the arm of the leather;
that is the kind of mistake I cannot get over.

They said it didn't matter, but it did. No way to fix it.
In paralysis, the question is do you stop
or just go forward.
As he faced the oncoming traffic, these are the things I think about.

Martha Remembering Sister Janina's Bones

At six thirty her children rolled their eyes.
You already told us that story.
Martha: tired, lingering and selfish,
walked off to the park.

She closed her eyes and saw a pattern of crosses
and beneath the geometry was a gorgeous magenta,
slightly darkened by the evening sky.

Somewhere near the end of summer and early fall,
she threw the flowers from their pots
near the pine and erected a geranium gravesite
where populations were thrown without ceremony in dark earth.

From Martha's Diary

Do we say this was not a chapbook, but a book.
Do we say I hadn't had a drop to drink when I became angry about the chutney.
Do we admit we lied for years.
Do we stand aside

and say it is nothing including
when we were seven and our Father finally called
and did not say your name or even
hello

When will it be enough to be graceful?

Alluring women are called to HR
and small lives confiscated to the cold killing floor
of machinist rooms.

Then will I tell you pumpkin people,
sometimes it is wise to complain
to the manager at the YMCA.

Let the chips fall chipmaster
as spring rain carefully falls..

Because there always is this sense of belonging.
Because the pink moon at the end of April is a promise.
Because Violet sings in the kitchen along with the chopping knife.
Because the mourning dove and lilies of the valley come up now that the azalea.
Because of fuchsia glory.

Absolution

The security guard offered Martha security;
a boat, three houses, in Natick, Orlando and New Hampshire,
said she was real nice.
I'm gonna need more than security
to get me through this ride, mister.

Her limit was three days, three pages of holy
writing where she could dip and take
the Eucharist and travel forward.
The dark look of the priest told her it was wrong,
but she persisted. What is a lie
but a graven image of something someone wanted
to have happened, made up.

Deep moth in late summer
how long is your life,
how long do you stay awake
suffering the moon?

Martha and the Traitor Jay

Angels are really here all along
                                    Rilke

She sat in the ruin of dawn.
Fear came from somewhere near
the ocean boathouse where she imagined
her children and worried about what she could afford
to sell, to give away, to lose.

The blue jay mocked her from the fence.
She dreamt of a svelte lover from
France who demanded nothing.
Martha said no to love, because
of what it cost her.

The blue jay shouted at her from within the green.
Please, he said, learn another song.

She was all along looking
for cupboard love loyalty,
a habit that liked her and her lover,
old hands touching young
love, against the grain.

Coastal Highway

On the 6th day of the pandemic
Martha woke to the CAW CAW CAW
of crows. One thought he was a God
and started barking. Eventually,
the others left in dismay and disgust,
for he split the nation in half.

In between the water that Moses parted,
there is a coastal highway,
one lane traffic one way.

Sometimes a man in a pick-up truck
will plunge into the sea
picking up speed as he moves through water.

I wonder why did she do it,
waste her life like a mild winter hedgehog?

Dog Poems

When the Dog is more Magnificent than the Man

His head lifted and most of it black, the dog walked
ahead of the man. The man in small tennis shoes
like a child holding back.
The dog led on muscled legs
elegant.
They may have been anywhere.
a deep forest where a German Shepherd
led a wounded man away from spies,
or in a cave with bats shimmering the walls,
or on in the Mediterranean against azure
skies under mosaic walls green, blue and white.

The dog walked on, and the man knew
it was beautiful. He even smiled
in secret knowledge that he was nothing
next to the immense beauty of dogeared intelligence
and grace that resided in the black paws.

The leash was a kind of connection of his soul
shining, beating, into a mere single strand
of gold barely visible,
a line of happiness saying *yes please*,
a child at a well,
          or a woman taking leave.
Were it not for the gold, I mean were it not for the god,
the man would not know a world such as this.

Girl with No Shoes

Red bangs flying, shamrock pajamas
on St. Paddy's Day, a young girl fleeing
down Quincy Avenue clutching a puppy
Spaniel, red headed, tongue wagging
on a sun-cold day.

I recognized her terror
as me hiding in a prickly evergreen.
Two fake deer stand over me on my left.
Wrists scratched. Why was the brother deer staring?

The apple tree in the yard was poisoned by Zepp.
I shouldn't eat the pie
that Annie, our babysitter, made for my birthday.
She told us (after all this time) about her brother
putting mice down her back at her farm
and how she screamed and howled
In the creases of her warm, oiled face small tears
slid, and I knew it wasn't funny
and reached for her small hand.

Panicked and Carrying a Dog

I saw another man carrying his dog
and began to wonder if this was a mass trend
to never let go and keep your dog close to your heart.

This one on a leash, small, white-russet.
The man slightly ill nourished.
Scraggy beard, young, unemployed with a certain panic
in both faces like the adolescent sneaking out
or guilty of some small crime while
carrying the odor of spaniel
and living room, or left-overs microwaved.

On the corner of Audubon and Arthur
I watched them turn into the alley
shadowed by (purple) lilac.

A short time later
they rounded the corner. This time
the man held the black, flimsy packy bag
six pack juggling against his heart.

His bounty, his keep, his prize and promise,
only the dog trotted on, impervious to virtue.

Sonya the Dog

We had a dog named Sonya Friedman after the town psychologist
(it was my mother's idea.)
The Christmas tree glittered
tragic.

Radishes sat in the crystal bobbed bowl,
nothing was turning out as planned.

In summer my brother and I went to work at Pentwater.
Sonya came too.

We swam in Lake Michigan as she barked
and clawed, trying to save us from recreation.

My room had a curtain in the middle
indicating the past presence of an invalid.
I decided it would be good to play the part
and went to the Thrift store to buy a dress from the 1950's,
Flouncy. Sequined. Three sizes too large.
Also, a nurses' outfit which I wore for years.

The dog was a mix of Shepherd and Lab.
She had a beauty mark like Liz Taylor,
black muzzle, ears and coat
the color of cinnamon.
Her paws were black.

My brother was the fry cook,
I the salad girl.
He bought a Pinto with a Givenchy leather interior.
It seemed odd to go to that trouble.
Never certain what happened to that dog
or where it slept.

(Our hearts can never be too far from what we love.)

Suddenly I Become the Dog

Feet melt to paws in the dust,
mouth slack open.

I have nothing to hide.
Chipmunk dead in the grass.
Did I do that?

His eyes weirdly peaceful
tail still fluffy
a small smile.

I don't remember it.
When time stopped, I was
chastised for recklessness

made decisions no longer justified.

In my youth I was a star shatterer.
Now I scatter black flies

left to my own devices,
sheltered and surrounded by flowers
forgotten or tamed.

What rubric against the sky,
Orion, lost love,
has caused this shift to silence?

My Aunt Gloria Carries the Dog

I saw my aunt in the future carrying the dog,
blond wig, Caesar cut, Pucci handbag.

Her dress was alive with lily green
pink, gladstone yellow. An A-frame
mini-dress white patent leather boots

and the dog was

well a dog.

She carried him along, the lamb.
He refused to see that she was
getting older
and would die
(how could he know or care?)

Little dog
Chinchilla boned
hard toothed by winter
easy to fool, careful in bed
luminous one;
the sun caught his teenage eye
near the forsythia and her yellow Cadillac.

I, Too, Have
a Chartreuse Cat

Forbidding Mourning

(After John Donne)

I

I woke with the heaviest air,
lumbered out of my box bed.
The windows shut. The songbirds gone.
Only garbage trucks clanging.

For the first time in months,
some child spoke to another.
His voice was a pearl,
no answer from the other side.

II

Jesus asked the woman at the well
for water. She asked him why
should she. He was a Jew after all.
She had no husband, but he told her to get her husband.

III

The child's hair was strawberry blond,
his boots sand
in the morning when the sun
lends its slant over the land.

(To go on gazing is a form of respect
for the unknown.)

IV

To think that the dream
you have dreamt for five years,

that the *little love god lying once asleep*
could ever still your hand with his cool watered hand
and bring you like a flamed flower alive.

V

Azalea, oh sweet fragrant lips
Oh sweet fuchsia
caress
May bird
sweet fuchsia kiss.

Ash Wednesday

On Watching a film with a Millennial

The next morning the sun was an orange ball
with a halo reaching out to the world
and I could no more think on Pasolini,

his pimps, whores and thieves
trying to forget my dream
where we were both going to teach a seminar

on beauty. It was vague. You had an outfit
and were in shape. You even had a bonnet.
The scholars were talking, and I was lost.

When I was young I found Dante and Pasolini.
They mimicked each other like European starlings.

Geese rose up in the sky in a triangle
honking and racing. It was as if my heart
stopped dead and I was no longer in the tower.

I dared not speak and say, this frame is important
Did you catch the Roman dialect?
What about her suede boots in summer?

Wintering bitter cold;
I've become a medieval lady in repose.

Glad Day (Albion!)

variation on a pantoum

First a small stone hit the windshield,
creating a star snowflake
in the glass, a teardrop,
but I barely noticed.

Creating a star snowflake in glass
It grew longer and longer.
But I barely noticed,
witch finger accusing.

It grew longer and longer.
Everything fragile ice splintering in moonlight
shattered thin like a witch's voice accusing.
Raising my voice in the driveway, I dropped the phone.

Fragile ice splintering in moonlight.
I reach into my coat pocket at the store for the phone, shards of glass,
a teardrop
of blood on my fingertip.
In the grocery line blood drips from my hand.

The man behind me curses, blood running down in teardrops.
In the car, ice rain hits the windshield.
The lines of my palm shatter.
Somewhere in the night

my cousin's framed blood-stained apron
with a trinity of blackbirds
drops to the floor,
something I did not notice

until the next day of light, the trinity of blackbirds
woven onto the blood-stained Russian World War 2 apron
dislodged from the frame I barely noticed.

Even blackbirds lose themselves in a bright day,
complete their open wings,
reflected in windshields.

Standing in the Willow

kintsugi

Stones and sea glass long neglected
and embedded in the hollow,
immobilized fossils
inside a green glazed bowl.

Grandmother's favorite color,
               pond moss
moss of the word
along the creek over stones,
old logistical guide.

My hands are like stones.
Moons of my fingernails
a memory of Monroe, Michigan and the convent.
The two faces if the Rouge River:
one of death where the cat, Jerome,
was found drowned, another
of ferns wide and light green.
She would climb down the bramble
to clip them for her side garden.

Now in the garage her smell comes to me a light must,
cigarettes and something I cannot name.
Her gardening gloves, white leather somewhat
Victorian, with a single blue stitch too elegant
and small for my hands. But I can work with her hand trowel,
potato fork, pruning shears, garden fork and the wooden loppers
for the tougher branches too high to reach.

Flying West

Did I shed the world?
My hand narrow, ringed and filled with strife,
worry, anxiety. When I read my palm
it said, *she ain't seen nothing yet.*

My pain was a house
to shut myself up in and disappear
into a window box of eternity.

If you get this, call me.
If you care to explain, put it in a song.
Shed light on the day.
Lifting into the pale pink to violet-blue
before you lose touch with that orange that kept
you like a girl among the tiger lillies.

Suddenly you are starved for the sunrise.

Grateful for this heartbeat
against the sky of indifferent vast
blue dusk rose
the cat's small blink, his yellow eye
shadowing my tired face in the garden where
you held my hand and sighed into my hair.

Eulogies for Small and Other Things

I. Smelt Brook

An army of frogs
soldiers of nowhere along the bank
of the smelt brook
leaving behind a small trail of dust.

A preserved carcass of a small frog lay
upside down.
Turning it over in the grass
upright, it black hollowed
intrinsic in the blue light of day
between the green trees
and the little moving stream over rocks.
There the stones measure the water
and twist the memory of twining snakes
and how they loved each other in the low grass.

II. Deep Blue Flower Pot II

Two dead mice found in a blue flower pot,
one more intact indicating
a longer drawn out death
with his lover already dead beside him.

Not shriveled but drawn, her body a half
circle, a moon.
Her spine was an arpeggio of angels.
Her delicate tail surrounds her like a question,
or a finger across lips.
Why couldn't they get
back to the first world?
Why couldn't they squeeze
through the hole they crept into?

I may have launched
the second pedestrian clay pot over them,
sealing their fate,
making their escape
impossible.

How long did he lie
there caught in his dream
after her smell became paper
and his young life gone.

III. Chipmunk in Driveway

It was June when the chipmunk
made his way through the yard
Only to be killed by the cat of the hours.

Large, plump, freckled and striped,
the chipmunk crawled in the driveway
quivering slightly.

The chipmunk was later seen in heaven
where he went after he crawled from the driveway
to the fence to die with his loved ones,
which is all we can ask
before entering the kingdom of God.

Acknowledgments

Artedolia: "Mamma Roma," "Cupboard Love Loyalty" collaboration with visual artist, Frank Navin, 2022

River Heron: "Absolution," 2022

Anit-Heroin Chic: "The Man Who Did Not Believe in Watches," 2021

First Literary Review East: "Opera Bag," 2020

Nixes Mate: "Martha Remembering Sister Janina's Bones," 2024

Spell Jar Press: "I Love a Motel in June, Don't You?" 2024

Lily Poetry Review, "Adorned with a Picnic Hat in a Black and White Photo," Visual poetry collaboration with Frank Navin 2024

Notes

Hamtramck, Michigan is a small enclave of Detroit. In the 20th century it was mostly populated by Polish-Americans who settled there.

The Relics and the Chalice are inspired by *Reed of God*, by Caryll Houselander. It is a book based the theological affirmations of Mary and the complex human condition.

The Ambassador Bridge is the longest international suspension bridge in the world. It connects Detroit to Canada.

Hough's Neck is a one square mile peninsula off Quincy, MA. The inhabitants are often referred to as 'neckars' or 'neck birds'. Nut Island is at the very tip of the peninsula.

"Valor is the better part of discretion" comes from the proverb: 'it is better to avoid a dangerous situation than to confront it'. Shakespeare, Falstaff, *Henry IV*.

The winter solstice of 2020 was the Great Conjunction meeting of Jupiter and Saturn. They were last seen the closest observable in 1226, the year Saint Francis of Assisi died.

The Immaculate Heart of Mary (IHM) is a convent located in Monroe, Michigan. Theresa Maxis founded the convent and school believing in the education of girls. She was born in Baltimore in 1810, of a Haitian mother and British father. She was well educated and articulate in both French and English. She was part of the early community of the Oblate Sisters of Providence, the first congregation of religious women of color in the world.

"The bones of Sister Mary Janina (Ya-nina) were unearthed from the basement cellar of Holy Rosary Catholic church in late 1918. It had been 11 years since the nun had gone missing. Father Edward Podlaszewski was the new priest who wanted to build a stylish church on the site. He had heard rumors from Bishop Edward Kozlowski and asked the sexton, Jacob Flees, to assist him on the late fall night. With lanterns and a potato fork in hand, the pair crept to the dirt floor under the wooden clapboard structure in the November duskiness." Martha Hayden, 2020, *The Restless Viking*.

George Van Tassel, aviator and Ufologist attempted to build a time machine in the Mojave Desert. *The Visionary State: A Journey Through California's Spiritual Landscape*, Michael Rauner with text by Erik Davis.

"Absolution" is taken from the short story by F.S. Fitzgerald.

Don Emilio Pucci, Marchese di Barsento was an Italian aristocrat, fashion designer and politician.

"A Valediction: Forbidding Mourning" by John Donne.

About the author

Gloria Monaghan is a Professor at Wentworth University. This is her seventh collection of poetry. Her poems have appeared in *Nixes Mate, NPR, Poem-a-Day, Lily Poetry Review, Mom Egg Review, Quartet* and *River Heron* among others. She has been nominated twice for the Pushcart Prize, as well as the Massachusetts Book Award and the Griffin Prize. She recently completed a film on painter Nancy Ellen Craig, which was accepted into the 2023 Provincetown Film Festival.

www.ingramcontent.com/pod-product-compliance
Lightning Source LLC
Chambersburg PA
CBHW070030030426
42335CB00017B/2368